Mama,

Some of the things mentioned in this book seems to come from a little kid — THEN I remembered that I was that little kid once.

You're the Best!

Love Dicky

For My Mom

You are a gift
straight from heaven!

With Love From

Dicky

Mom, You're Heaven Sent
Copyright 2002 by Zondervan
ISBN 0-310-80315-2

Compiler and Project Manager: Molly C. Detweiler
Design: Kris Nelson
Illustration: Kallen Godsey

Printed in China
03 04 05/HK/5 4 3 2

Mom, You're Heaven Sent

inspirio™

The gift group of Zondervan

I Love You, Mom!

Mom's smiles can brighten any moment,
Mom's hugs put joy in all our days,
Mom's love will stay with us forever
and touch our lives in precious ways.

The values you've taught,
the care you've given,
and the wonderful love you've shown,
have enriched my life,
and blessed my days
in more ways than can be known.
I love you, Mom!

AUTHOR UNKNOWN

Your love has given me
great joy
and encouragement.

PHILEMON 1:7

Famous Words from Mom

A little soap and water never killed anybody.

Don't go out with a wet head, you'll catch cold.

Always wear clean underwear
in case you get in an accident.

Clean up after yourself!

Don't sit too close to the television;
it'll ruin your eyes.

Be good.

If you keep making that face
it'll freeze that way.

Don't eat that, you'll get worms!

Money doesn't grow on trees.

Don't put that in your mouth,
you don't know where it's been.

Close the door! You don't live in a barn.

Don't talk with your mouth full!

Enough is enough!

"I don't know" is NOT an answer.

If you can't say something nice,
don't say anything at all.

If God had wanted you to have holes
in your ears (eyebrows, tongue, etc.)
He would have put them there!

If you could stay out last night,
you can get up this morning.

If you're too full to finish your dinner,
you're too full for dessert.

Never try on anyone else's glasses
or you'll go blind.

When you have your own house
then you can make the rules!

If you're too sick to go to school,
you're too sick to play outside.

You will ALWAYS be my baby.

I will always love you—no matter what.

For all the times you stayed up
When my tummy was upset
And all the nights you made up
Stories, because I wasn't sleepy yet
For all the things you gave up
To make sure my needs were met
Mom, this little girl you raised up
Will never, ever your love forget!

MOLLY C. DETWEILER

A mother's heart holds many charms
And love is ever in her arms.
And in her eyes a faith divine,
And home is you, Mother mine.

AUTHOR UNKNOWN

God gives us friends—
and that means much;
but far above all others,
the greatest of
His gifts to earth
was when
He thought of mothers.

ANONYMOUS

Mom's Brownie Recipe

Remove teddy bear from oven
and preheat oven to 375 degrees.

Melt 1 cup of margarine in saucepan.

Remove teddy bear from oven and tell Junior, "No, no."

Add margarine to 2 cups of sugar.

Take shortening can away from Junior and clean cupboards.

Measure 1/3-cup cocoa.

Take shortening can away from Junior again and bathe cat.

Apply antiseptic and bandages to scratches sustained
while removing shortening from cat's tail.

Mix 4 eggs, 2 tsp. vanilla, and 1 1/2 cups sifted flour.

Take smoldering teddy bear from oven and
open all doors and windows for ventilation.

Measure 1 tsp. salt, 1/2 cup nuts.

Mix all ingredients well.

Take telephone away from Billy and assure
party on the line the call was a mistake.
Call operator and attempt to have
direct dialed call removed from bill.

Let cat out of refrigerator.

Pour mixture into well-greased 9x13-inch pan.

Bake 25 minutes.

Rescue cat and take razor away from Billy. Explain
that you have no idea if shaved cats will sunburn.
Put cat outside while he's still able to run away.

Take the teddy bear out of the broiler
and throw it away—far away.

Add 1/3-cup milk, dash of salt, and boil,
stirring constantly for 2 minutes.

Answer door and apologize to neighbor for Billy
having stuck a garden hose in man's front door
mail slot. Promise to pay for ruined carpet.

Tie Billy to clothesline.

Remove burned brownies from oven.

My Mother

My Mother,
my friend so dear
throughout my life
you're always near.
A tender smile
to guide my way
You're the sunshine
to light my day.

AUTHOR UNKNOWN

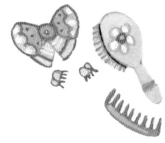

Mother

You filled my days with rainbow lights,
Fairytales and sweet dream nights,
A kiss to wipe away my tears,
Gingerbread to ease my fears.

You gave the gift of life to me
And then in love, you set me free.
I thank you for your tender care,
For deep warm hugs and being there.

I hope that when you think of me
A part of you
You'll always see.

AUTHOR UNKNOWN

Mom's Dictionary

BOTTLE-FEEDING: An opportunity for Daddy to get up at 2 A.M., too.

DUMBWAITER: One who asks if the kids would care to order dessert.

FAMILY PLANNING: The art of spacing your children the proper distance apart to keep you on the edge of financial disaster.

FEEDBACK: The inevitable result when the baby doesn't appreciate the strained carrots.

FULL NAME: What you call your child when you're mad at him.

HEARSAY: What toddlers do when anyone mutters a dirty word.

INDEPENDENT: How we want our children to be as long as they do everything we say.

May you be blessed by the Lord,
the maker of heaven and earth.

PSALM 115:15

Life Lessons
(Only a Mom Can Teach)

My mother taught me...

about ANTICIPATION
"Just wait until your father gets home."

about RECEIVING
"You are going to get it when we get home!"

to MEET A CHALLENGE
"What were you thinking? Answer me when
I talk to you! ... Don't talk back to me!"

LOGIC
"If you fall out off that swing and break your
neck, you're not going to the store with me."

YIP!

AGRICULTURE
"If you don't stop swallowing those
seeds watermelons will grow out your ears."

to THINK AHEAD
"If you don't pass your spelling test,
you'll never get a good job."

to BECOME AN ADULT
"Eat your vegetables, or you'll never grow up."

HUMOR
"When that lawn mower cuts off your toes,
don't come running to me."

about my ROOTS
"Do you think you were born in a barn?"

And my all time favorite ... JUSTICE
"One day you'll have kids, and I hope they turn
out just like you. Then you'll see what it's like."

Real Moms

Real mothers don't eat quiche;
who has time to make quiche?

Real mothers know that when they are
missing a kitchen utensil it can probably
be found in the sandbox.

Real mothers often have sticky floors,
filthy ovens, and happy kids.

Real mothers know that dried play dough doesn't
come out of shag carpets.

Real mothers don't want to know
what the vacuum just sucked up.

Real mothers sometimes ask "Why me?"
and get their answer when a little voice says,
"Because I love you best."

Real mothers know that a child's growth is not
measured by height or years or grade. It is marked
by the progression of Ma-ma to Mommy to Mom.

Thanks, Mom, for being a real mother to me.

AUTHOR UNKNOWN

My mother's love,
a precious gift,
Sent from
heaven above.
Her prayer for me
is Mom's amen
To God's own
gift of love.

AUTHOR UNKNOWN

Kids' Wisdom

No matter how hard you try,
you cannot baptize cats.

If your sister hits you,
don't hit her back. They always
catch the second person.

Never ask your three-year-old
brother to hold a tomato.

You can't trust dogs to
watch your food.

Reading what people write on
desks can teach you a lot.

YIP!

Don't sneeze when someone
is cutting your hair.

Puppies still have bad breath
even after eating a Tic-Tac.

Never hold a Dustbuster
and a cat at the same time.

School lunches stick to the wall.

You can't hide a piece of broccoli
in a glass of milk.

Don't wear polka-dot underwear
under white shorts.

The best place to be when you are sad
is in Mommy's lap.

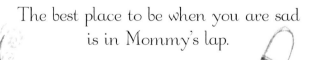

Moms can
always hear
what their
children
don't say.

A Mother's Love

There are times when only a Mother's love
Can understand our tears,
Can soothe our disappointments
And calm all of our fears.

There are times when only a Mother's love
Can share the joy we feel
When something we've dreamed about
Quite suddenly is real.

There are times when only a Mother's faith
Can help us on life's way
And inspire in us the confidence
We need from day to day.

For a Mother's heart and a Mother's faith
And a Mother's steadfast love
Were fashioned as the angels'
And sent from God above.

AUTHOR UNKNOWN

Mother's Day Cards

Dear Mother: I'm going to make dinner for you
for Mother's Day. It's going to be a surprise.
P.S. I hope you like pizza and popcorn.

YOUR DAUGHTER, ANGIE H., AGE 8

Dear Mother: Here is a box of candy I bought you
for Mother's Day. It is very good candy
because I already ate three of the pieces.

LOVE, MARCY C., AGE 8

Dear Mother: I got you a turtle for Mother's Day.
I hope you like the turtle I got you this year for
Mother's Day better than the snake I got you
for Mother's Day last year.

YOUR SON, ROBBY H., AGE 8

Dear Mother: Here are two aspirins.
Have a happy Mother's Day.

LOVE, CARRIE H., AGE 8

Parents are the pride of their children.

PROVERBS 17:6

25

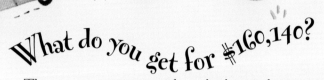

What do you get for $160,140?

The government recently calculated the cost of raising a child from birth to 18 and came up with $160,140 for a middle-income family. Talk about sticker shock! That doesn't even touch college tuition! But $160,140 isn't so bad if you break it down. It translates into $8,896.66 a year, $741.38 a month or $171.08 a week. That's a mere $24.44 a day—just over a dollar an hour. Still, you might think the best financial advice says don't have children if you want to be rich. The truth is it's just the opposite. There's no way to put a price tag on:

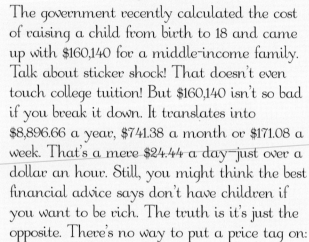

- Feeling a new life move for the first time and seeing the bump of a knee rippling across your skin.

- Having someone cry, "It's a boy!" or shout, "It's a girl!" then hearing the baby wail.

- Counting all 10 fingers and toes for the first time.

- Feeling the warmth of fat cheeks against your breast.
- Cupping an entire head in your palm.
- Making out "da-da" or "ma-ma" from all the cooing and gurgling.
- Naming rights—first, middle and last.
- Glimpses of God every day.
- Giggles under the covers every night.
- More love than your heart can hold.
- Butterfly kisses and Velcro hugs.
- Endless wonder over rocks, ants, clouds, and warm cookies.
- A hand to hold, usually covered with jam.
- A partner for blowing bubbles, flying kites, building sand castles, and skipping down the sidewalk in the pouring rain.
- Someone to laugh yourself silly with no matter what the boss said or how your stocks performed that day.

For $160,140 you never have to grow up.

- You get to fingerpaint, carve pumpkins, play hide-and-seek, catch lightning bugs and never stop believing in Santa Claus. You have an excuse to keep reading the adventures of Piglet and Pooh, to watch Saturday morning cartoons, to go to Disney movies, and to wish on stars.

- You get to frame rainbows, hearts, and flowers under refrigerator magnets and collect spray painted noodle wreaths for Christmas, and handprints set in clay for Mother's Day.

- You get to be a hero just for retrieving a Frisbee off the garage roof, taking the training wheels off the bike, removing a splinter, filling the wading pool, and coaxing a wad of gum out of bangs. In the eyes of a child, you rank right up there with God.

- You have the power to heal a boo-boo, scare away monsters from under the bed, patch a broken heart, police a slumber party, ground them forever and love them without limits, so one day they will, like you, love without counting the cost.

What an investment you've made—and what priceless dividends you receive!

*A rich child
often sits
in a
poor mother's lap.*

SPANISH PROVERB

I Said a Mother's Prayer for You

I said a Mother's prayer for you
to thank the Lord above
for blessing me with a lifetime
of your tenderhearted love.
I thanked God for the caring
you've shown me through the years,
for the closeness we've enjoyed
in time of laughter and of tears.
And so, I thank you from the heart
for all you've done for me
and I bless the Lord for giving me
the best mother there could be!

AUTHOR UNKNOWN

THE LORD BLESSES
THE HOME OF THE RIGHTEOUS.

PROVERBS 3:33

I WAS YOUNG AND NOW I AM OLD,
YET I HAVE NEVER SEEN
THE RIGHTEOUS FORSAKEN
OR THEIR CHILDREN BEGGING BREAD.
THEY ARE ALWAYS GENEROUS
AND LEND FREELY;
THEIR CHILDREN WILL BE BLESSED.

PSALM 37:25–26

SCHOOL
ZONE

Mom and Me

Best friends forever
mom and me
Picking flowers and
climbing trees.
A shoulder to cry on,
secrets to share
Warm hearts, and hands
that really care.

AUTHOR UNKNOWN

Thank You, Mom,

For being my comforter, provider, chef, nurse,
teacher, encourager, friend, mentor, coach,
trainer, confidant, disciplinarian, pastor,
advocate, and defender ... but most of all,
for just being my Mommy!

MOLLY C. DETWEILER

A KINDHEARTED WOMAN GAINS RESPECT.

PROVERBS 11:16

More from Mom's Dictionary

PUDDLE: A small body of water that draws other small bodies wearing dry shoes into it.

STERILIZE: What you do to your first baby's pacifier by boiling it and to your last baby's pacifier by blowing on it.

STOREROOM: The distance required between the supermarket aisles so that children in shopping carts can't quite reach anything.

TEMPER TANTRUMS: What you should keep to a minimum so as to not upset the children.

TOP BUNK: Where you should never put a child wearing Superman jammies.

TWO-MINUTE WARNING: When the baby's face turns red and she begins to make those familiar grunting noises.

VERBAL: Able to whine in words.

WHODUNIT: None of the kids that live in your house.

WHOOPS: An exclamation that translates roughly into "get a sponge."

Many women do noble things,
but you surpass them all.

PROVERBS 31:29

Here's to Mommies

I shared breakfast in bed with a handsome young man today. Of course, the breakfast consisted of a bowl of oatmeal and leftover cookie crumbs found between the sheets. The handsome young man is about thirty-four inches tall and only gets excited at the sight of purple dinosaurs, toy trucks, and French Fries.

I also got to take a relaxing stroll in the woods. Of course I had to look for frogs and lizards, and stop to smell the dandelions along the way.

I successfully washed one load of laundry, moved the load that was in the washer into the dryer, and the dryer load into the basket. The load that was in the basket is now spread out on the bed, awaiting my bedtime decision to actually put the clothes away or merely move them to the top of the dresser.

I read two or three classics. Of course,
Dickens and Shakespeare cannot take credit
for these works, as we have moved on to the works
of Seuss and Sendak.

In between, I dusted, wiped, rearranged and
organized. I kissed away the "owies" and washed
away the tears. I scolded, praised, hugged, and
had my patience tested, all before noon.

The point is, that today I got to watch my children take another step on the great journey of
Life, and I even got to point out some of the sites
along the way. As challenging as parenthood is, it
is also equally rewarding, because we are using all
our wisdom, our talent and skills to help forge a
new person. It is this person, these people, who, in
turn, will use their gifts to create.

So every nursery rhyme I recite, every swing
I push, every little hand I hold is SOMETHING!
And I did it today.

AUTHOR UNKNOWN

Sometimes things get a little lost in the translation when it comes to teaching little ones about the Bible!

Bible Lessons from Kids

In the first book of the Bible, Guinessis, God got tired of creating the world, so he took the Sabbath off.

Lot's wife was a pillar of salt by day, but a ball of fire by night.

Moses led the Hebrews to the Red Sea, where they made unleavened bread, which is bread without any ingredients.

The first commandment was when Eve told Adam to eat the apple.

The fifth commandment is to humor thy father and mother.

Moses died before he ever reached Canada.

The greatest miracle in the Bible is when Joshua told his son to stand still and he obeyed him.

David was a Hebrew king skilled at playing the liar. He fought with the Finklesteins, a race of people who lived in Biblical times.

*M*ost Wonderful

*O*verwhelmingly Sweet

*T*errifically Gifted

*H*eart Pure as Gold

*E*ver Patient and Caring

*R*esponsible for So Much Joy

MOLLY C. DETWEILER

Mom's Resumé

Being a mom requires so many skills that it would make for a very impressive resume!

EXCELLENT AT MULTI-TASKING: can answer the phone, pick up toys, stir dinner and hold crying baby all while making a mental grocery list to be written down later.

EXPERIENCED IN MEDICAL DIAGNOSIS AND TREATMENT: knows the difference between a nervous bellyache and the beginning of the flu by the look on a child's face; many hours of surgical experience (removing splinters from toes, peas from nostrils and specks of dust from eyes).

WELL-VERSED IN CLASSIC LITERATURE: can recite many works from memory including the complete works of "Dr. Seuss" and "The Little Engine That Could."

CULINARY ARTIST: able to hide any vegetable in layers of potatoes for ease of consumption; received high marks for perfect balance of peanut butter and jelly in sandwiches; has almost magical ability to make an all new meal completely from the week's leftovers.

COUNSELOR AND CONFLICT MEDIATOR: swiftly settles disputes over property rights between warring factions (i.e. Two sisters, one doll); highly skilled in grief management through hug therapy and liberal administering of warm cookies.

MOLLY C. DETWEILER

Life began with waking up and loving my mother's face.

GEORGE ELIOT

THE UNFADING BEAUTY OF
A GENTLE AND QUIET SPIRIT ...
IS OF GREAT WORTH
IN GOD'S SIGHT.

1 PETER 3:4

She's Just Perfect

A small boy invaded the lingerie section of a big department store and shyly presented his problem to the salesclerk. "I want to buy my mom a slip as a present," he said, "but I don't know what size she wears."

The clerk said, "It would help to know if your mom is short or tall, skinny or not so skinny." "She's just perfect," beamed the little boy, so the clerk wrapped up a size 6 for him.

Two days the later Mom came into the store herself and changed it to a size 12.

AUTHOR UNKNOWN

Mother love is the fuel that
enables a normal human being
to do the impossible.

AUTHOR UNKNOWN

The Guinness Book of World Records
reported that in Tampa, Florida, on April
24, 1960, a 123-pound woman lifted one end
of a 3,600 lb. (1.60 tons) station wagon,
which, after the collapse of a jack, had fall-
en on top of her son. A mother's love can
truly move mountains!

ANONYMOUS

LOVE ALWAYS PROTECTS, ALWAYS TRUSTS,
ALWAYS HOPES, ALWAYS PERSEVERES.

1 CORINTHIANS 13:7

Love never fails.

1 CORINTHIANS 13:8

The Angel

Once upon a time there was a child ready to be born. The child asked God, "They tell me you are sending me to earth tomorrow, but how am I going to live there being so small and helpless?"

God replied, "Among the many angels, I chose one for you. Your angel will be waiting for you and will take care of you."

The child further inquired, "But tell me, here in heaven I don't have to do anything but sing and smile to be happy."

God said, "Your angel will sing for you and will also smile for you every day. And you will feel your angel's love and be very happy."

Again the child asked, "And how am I going to be able to understand when people talk to me if I don't know the language?"

God said, "Your angel will tell you the most beautiful and sweet words you will ever hear, and with much patience and care, your angel will teach you how to speak."

"And what am I going to do when I want to talk to you?"

God said, "Your angel will place your hands together and will teach you how to pray."

"I've heard that on Earth there are bad men. Who will protect me?"

God said, "Your angel will defend you even if it means risking its life."

"But I will always be sad because I will not see you anymore."

God said, "Your angel will always talk to you about me and will teach you the way to come back to me, even though I will always be next to you."

At that moment there was much peace in heaven, but voices from Earth could be heard and the child hurriedly asked, "God, if I am to leave now, please tell me my angel's name."

"Her name is not important. You will simply call her Mom."

All I am
or hope to be
I owe to
my angel
mother.

ABRAHAM LINCOLN